MW01243144

Message from the Daughters:

Sent from the Midheaven via fire and brimstone

By

Ayesha Hakim

Copyright © 2021 by Ayesha Hakim

All rights reserved. No part of this publication may be reproduced, distributed, or transmitted in any form or by any means, including photocopying, recording, or other electronic or mechanical methods, without prior written permission of the publisher, except in the case of brief quotations embodied in critical reviews and certain other noncommercial uses permitted by copyright law.

Printed in the United States of America.

Message from the Daughters:

Sent from the Midheaven via fire and brimstone

By

Ayesha Hakim

Cover photo art: *Sanian* by Laura Ferreira

Interior Art: Izrael Marcellus

Book format design and layout: David Colon

www.ayeshahakim.com

Dedication

To Nia & Divya:

I am forever grateful for your breath, for it has kept the message alive inside me.

And to Josh:

Your being keeps me strong. Understand the message, and you'll understand the woman.

And to Joe da Costa:

Special thanks for helping to unravel me just enough, making it possible to deliver my message.

And to the daughters whose message is en route or has yet to be written:

You are the mirror that reflects light when I am surrounded by darkness. I see you. I hear you. I love you. I thank you.

And to Mommy:

I Am because You Are.

Table of Contents

Chapter 1
Daleth 434
(I came. I saw. And lo and behold! I was disappointed.)

Beyond the Matrix

Mouth wrinkles and crows feet
mark the ending of
a trip thru dimensions.
Now we enter new beginnings

with tears, laughter, a
cautious abortion and then back
to the Roots in the Red Sea.
Quick journey. Now another

dairy cow feeds in the pasture.
Misunderstandings and
new beliefs, endings of sunsets and
smoke-filled chimneys of

burning flowers are our energy.
Death camps and
the desolate starting over
again act as our buffer.

Continuous life in this atmosphere
leads us to travel again.
Twinkle, twinkle, starlight,
and then dead be the stars.

Knowing and forgetting
cigar smoke and Hitchcock films
champagne in beer bottles
and laughter of mute children,

Adam and Noah and Jesus,
families and loneliness
and family again.
Stop the pain and then

start the song.
Remix it into the next
continuous beginning.
Next stop—

Earth—*again.*

Town Meetings and Congressional Conference

Across the horizon, a movement has ended
And new times are punctuated
With conflicting laws and new beliefs,
While parallel lines communicate
With creatures from the kingdom of sulfur and ultra rays.

One says, "Let's talk about flowers and trees
And sun-filled beaches.
And let's be inhabitants of stability's palace.
And we will mimic the brilliant seekers of peace and love
And turn a deaf ear to extreme murmurs that lead
Into a prelude of songs from dead sparrows."

But the magenta terrestrial who came through this crowd
Became disoriented and boarded
The first traveling comet back to its galaxy.
Obviously, the weight of a feather now equals a megaton of dust
(Dust from the comet's travel, pass this earth).

And it is inevitable that the abolition of those parallel lines
Will leave us inert and baffled and baffled and inert.
But if we download mankind and upload humankind
And propel a new action toward the historic gods
And choreograph a new dance for the melodrama,
The fibers in those lines will keep giving life in small doses.

Society's Disclaimer

All heads in opposition
Democrats and Republicans
Just boys playin' cowboys and Indians
Politics they be kickin'
Callin' for a nation to—*what?*
Peace? Equality? Justice?
Words bouncing off echoes
And placing lies gently behind our ears—

Fabrication

New pieces of metal—sharp and dangerous
Placed in hands of the unloved leading to
Jail cells and prison walls
Stones and swords
Gangs and wars
Piercing the heart and soul of Peace
Like when stolen birds slay the twin brothers in the new city
Or prior heat melting flesh off bodies across the waters—

Provocation

Men play the hierarchy
Disguised as prophets and such
Spewing words that are
Soothing like whispers from roots of the oak tree
The *Hellbringer* sings a tune
And his DNA finds you
With a sledgehammer
Innocence is taken away and replaced by everlasting questions
of—*Why?*—

Immorality
Arms of the dollar get weaker and shorter
Greed's limbs get longer and stronger
Gripping the life in the ghetto
Causing mayhem in the streets
But a guest of honor at dinner parties in the suburbs
Where they fancy themselves with talks of nothing but—
bullshit—

Insatiability
Lies and anger and wickedness and confusion and injustice and
voraciousness—

In Gods We Trust—
Fruition

Since Then

Banging from the East
Thoughts and fire run amok
Confused with the Holy endowment from the horizon
Your war is a sound from large broken bells
Sounds that cringe the ears of unborn angels
The children are disappearing amongst the sparkle of victory
And all are confused by your inspiration—

Where are the rulers and lords from the promise?
Lost in the games from their youth
Shoot! Shoot! Bang! Bang!
You're out! I won!
Time to come in, boys, supper's ready.
Only they don't all return
Lights out, and then inspiration comes—

Who is saddened by the lost gods now?
Prayers continue to pour in from the saints
While media prophets keep tainting the message
The search for true meaning is endless, tiring, and aggravating
Tiring like walking an endless dark tunnel
Aggravating because the carrot is dangled before the hungry
My soul comforts in a peace—
A peace from an inspiration that comes only from dreaming—

But mangled
And since then, we've been troubled
I know of a world where stillness inspires
I know of a place where people greet with sincerity of thought
I know of a place where "love" is not an afterthought
This place inspiration flows

7

Giant Little Steps

Moon trips
Homelessness

Metal birds
Cancer cells

Microchips
Hungry children

World wide web
World wide war

We've done a lot, haven't we?

Chapter 2
Arrival and Attendance
(Your presence has been noted.)

Lost Glasses

I saw a white bird

Flying in the sky

I don't know if it was a dove

Or a pigeon

I didn't have my glasses

It looked real pretty

Flying in the sky

Over the projects

Where my mother lived

I don't think it was a dove

A Story by a Little Girl
Interpreted by a Woman

While feeling the fist in her throat and witnessing fire on the bed
of waters

I painted the color God on cathedral ceilings for her to gaze
upon

When her dolls and will to speak were taken away

I gathered words for her to play with

Her glass was left empty

But I make it appear three-quarters full

Once, we both shouted to old drunken ears who said it would be
okay

Only to be sent back to the monster's ball

I feel nothing, but the little girl feels everything

The entire "nothing" is confused, and the "everything" is
amongst the fire

Intertwined, we both fall in and out of life's doors

The little girl is forever apprehensive

And I am weary of this endless dance with demons

And once the institution came in with microscopic lenses on

their eyes

Frightening the little girl who had so much to tell

But I stepped up, feeling the little girl tremble

And said, "It's okay now, I'll take care of her"

You see, the little girl may be afraid,

But I will protect her at all costs

Where do we begin to unravel fears when they're all around?

"Find the bag and move dust off the clouds,"

Whispered Angels at the Inn as they helped

Loop echoes with fine acoustics for the little girl

And with weaved hands

Prevented us both from falling into the grave

And made our room safe to wail

The little girl is asleep, and I am drained

Wondering if tomorrow we will find a way to tell our story

Knowing we will fight monsters again

Angels at the Inn help us both to keep flight in our dreams

As we rest peacefully through the night

Temporarily secure amongst the unknown shadows

Bubblegirl and Doubledutch
(for Querida—when I was little)

"Mama, can I go outside and play Doubledutch?"
Mama sleep, so now I stay away from confusion.

"Mama, can I go outside and play hopscotch?"
Mama sleep, so now I don't throw my pebbles too far.

"Mama, can I go outside and play tag?"
Mama sleep, so now I'm never "it."

"Mama, can I go outside and play hide-n-go-seek?"
Mama sleep, so now I hide from life.

"Mama, can I go outside; it's sunny today?"
Mama sleep, so now I'm comfortable in the dark.

"Mama, can I go outside to breathe, goddammit?!"
Grounded, just for the thought.

I stay inside all the time now, peeking out my window,

Living in my bubble, created by Mama.

Accepting My 'F' in Patience Lesson: 101

standing in a New World Chaos
time is thick, and the air is
insufficient. She moves slowly.
her heart beats hesitantly

and the salt in her eyes loses
its acidity as she climbs over every
mountain looking for that rainbow
that's supposed to be hers.

> and
> she looks in the lowest valleys
> and
> turns over the heaviest boulders
> and
> she never gives up
> and
> she finds it
> and
> it just ain't *enuf.*

she falls to the bottom of
secular situations that force
her on waiting lists that
close just as she shows up.

she has doubts about her existence
in this place for she is forever
haunted by her induction to
the Hall of Trauma or should we

say *life*. hating this worldliness
and hating this dimension and its
uncaring stillness that causes her
pain like seven trillion sickle cells

in her tiny veins or taking on
womanhood at age three. she waits
for someone to appear and chase
the beasts away, but no one ever comes.

> and
> no one says here is the key
> and
> no one teaches her how to cry
> and
> now she is uncertain if it is safe to weep
> and
> sleep eases her every thought
> and
> daytime awakens the monster's shadows.

so her soul remains trapped in a body
that can't move about, and she begins
to die cause this stillness acts as
kryptonite to the superb woman

she can be. she is convinced to
forsake dreams that traveled with her
and will no longer remain baptized
in trauma 'cause her rainbow just ain't here.

> and
> she is a soul of the Daughters

15

and
she still wants to fly *(although her wings are clipped)*
and
this life won't allow her
and
sad endings will not elude her
and so—
Sister Maya? I'll take that cool drink of water now.

Defender of Me

(for Robin)

She screams in a voice that is silent
His voice is thunderous and
Unpleasant and his smile, frightening

It happened to her as a child
Swinging in the branches
Baptized three times in trauma

Past memories lay deep in the grooves of her mind
But its intricacies protect her from falling
Into an ending sleep

Paper and pen gave her life
And fantasies kept
An unseen smile on her face

Invisible at home and abroad
She stayed in the safe parts of her thoughts
While waiting for words to come play with her

She protects her words
As a mother protects her young
She became a defender of me

Promises of ending the burning fire on her skin
Were fleeting, but the words came with
More syllables and more life

Soon, what was written became
Of one accord with her conscious and

17

Assurance of self was conceived but not yet birthed

After two decades of betrayal
Hopes to stop the rough rain
Are near because words flow like thick snow in the night

His presence can no longer devour
Her blessings that impregnate her being
New pleasures from words feed on her mental

She becomes a scribe to the true Self
Words taught her what she did not know
And allowed her to feel what she could not feel before

She protects her words and mind
As a mother protects her young
She became a defender of me

Turmoil was led to the house of rest
And bountiful threats were denied their unique canvas
As keys to her doors were melted and made into a spear

Shadows of her nemesis are now
Regulated like an iris diaphragm
She is mindful of self-imposed prohibitions

Like a blistered wound, drained and now healed
She received the prize although
It felt like new grout on an old tiled wall

Feeling human now, she wears a smile that can be seen
And words and thoughts effloresced

In the new haven that is rightfully hers

They come when she is happy or angry or learning
And when she is remembering her journey
And deciding which one to take now

She protects her words and mind and Self
As a mother protects her young
She became a defender of me

Strength, Come Hither
(for Eva)

Her cries beckon

from the crevices of darkness.

I hear her wailing even when

the thunder roars outside.

Her tongue cannot be found,

and she is thirsty from her search.

Her dwelling place speaks of

her existence, and I cannot deny

the story it writes. Why can't she leave

and disappear among those waves?

She beckons for strength, and

her frame can no longer hold her sorrow.

Don't cry for her yesterday!

Hold back the laughter until

she is just dust again. It was

once found. But now she is forever

searching. Please watch over her words

and shelter her being and remember

her song and answer her cry

and show her the way

and take her there.

Clasping in the Storm
(for Anjunelly)

Establishing new boundaries with shiny teeth and smiling hearts
comes to a halt
When stolen moments lead me to formulate suspicions of my
worthiness
My indignation rises as I encounter new propositions in
jurisdictions unfamiliar with my mental
My silence screams loud in this place
Where new hopes turn into old confusion
And laughter transforms into rivers
Should tears fall from my eyes tonight
They will flood the gates of my hell
Scattering the fire like wool blankets over a bed of feathers
Sister Anj, the storm is coming!

Matriculating errors hunt me down on this upward journey to
Golgotha
Instructing me to form self-inhibitions
As my emotions go under trial and error
City lights fade in esteem's eye, causing
Children to blow leaves off newborn trees
And growth spurts among cynical souls send obstacles to the
redeeming goddess
When the red baron makes his appearance on the turbulent ship
Sister Anj, the storm is here!

Indigo child I am, a creature of continuous birth
Through this labor, new dreams are born
Changing destinies that bring me closer to reality's level

Pasteurized bodies and gothic-styled candles light my way
through this darkness
But I am glad to be barefoot on the broken glass and jagged
stones that tear into my flesh
'Cause I can feel!
Torn between hating this dimension and loving the challenge—
Sister Anj, the storm has left!

Stolen cookies off white picnic tables has more meaning than
naught
And hydrated chrysanthemums are seen through the windows I
choose
Loving the breeze that caresses my skin and keeps me dreaming
of days of flight—
Shiloh! The clouds are gathering again.

Chapter 3
Nuclear Reactions

('Cuz shit happens when mixing the wrong reagents in the Büchner flask.)

Got Love?

Love had me sore
But I wanted more and more
Of this thing called love

It sparks the fire
That elevates me higher
Designed to be cherished
Like a newly opened flower
I find my peace in love

Took a sip from the Royal Chalice
Felt the sex beckon us
Then I glare
You stare
At me
It felt like love's conception
The greatest you
Meeting the greatest me
It was orgasmic

Left you secure with my words
Like a parable
Gave you wisdom
Direction
A lesson
To unlock your potential and fly

And you flew
Away
With my love source
Changed our course
And started something new

The unjust changed the word spoken
And you scorned me
Had four cases pendin'
Two be pregnant
Showed ya ass at the scene
Claimed to be a king
How can that be so when I have reign?

Pardon your confidence, son
Work in ya place, son
And don't dispute my message

Love had me sore
But I wanted more and more
Of this thing called love
Which now turned into aggression
This aggression took on a life of its own
And now I am
Different
A slave to its ideas
Against those who oppress me
I revolt justly

I do you like Creon
Destroy you with the poison
Bring down your Kingdom
Cause you to perish what you earn, son

Then like Medea, the Greek goddess
Leave you empty
Fly off in the chariot
Hear the Chorus callin' me out

27

Women of Corinth
Edgin' and walkin' about
I ended it all
And still remain tall
Because

I birth the sea
I still the wind
I direct the moon
I inform the sun to rise and how bright to shine
I am
Blissful, I am
Beautiful Oasis
The sharp unusual flavor
Of the world's greatest spiritual force

Never separate me from my supremacy
'Cause I reign with the deity
During any desperate hour
Tap into my Chakra
Increase me to the 10th power
My strength is locked for life

Take my 4 destiny and change the world
Turn love into passion
Passion into aggression
Aggression into creativity
And watch me exhale
(Through this pain)

Love had me sore—

But I *want* more and more

And more
Of this thing called love

Got love?

Ghost Giver
(for Maria)

Um, excuse me, but can I ask you a question?
If greed has left you friendless
And her heartless, what will the maggots feed on?
And if I'm so merciless to love
Will you admit to mistaking me for a dung beetle?
And are your anger and feelings of regret
Supposed to be the fuel I live on?
Since I'm now forever graced with suspicion,
I guess this means you've both won.
Well, congratulations.

Ms. Blacque Widow
(for Div aka Chris)

Ms. B stays busy in her web
She's spinnin' and spinnin'
Creations of wisdom
Movin' to beats of her own drum
Her flow givin' birth to words that cure
Any ailment that exist in your dome
As usual, she's interrupted—
    By *dude*
        The boy who thinks he's all that
            Blind to the fact
                That his game is whack
                  And tired y'all!
                    C'mon, we've
                heard it all before
                    Who you
                be?

                  Where you from?
                  Where your man
            at?
              But Ms. B continues spinnin'
            As dude continues gamin'
        And seekin' to inhabit her web
      He chases her black legs
And begs and begs and begs
    Finally, she lets 'em know
        How her story goes:
            My flow ignites a spark
            My bite is worse than my bark
            I'm bossy, impatient

31

Temperamental
But took time out for love
Some time ago
But dude didn't heed love's rule
Instead, he decided to choose
Games that I don't play
Put up with that fool every day
Until my poison became mature
And then I gave my heart the cure
Bit into his nonsense
And extracted all his excuses
And then I kept it movin'
Now I just keep spinnin'
and spinnin'
and spinnin'
As she said all this
He didn't hear it
His eyes was busy roamin'
Up and down her physical
Movin' across her body
Finding their way on her
Lips, Tits, Hips
Now,
she's gettin' high
of
f the
power she
possess
To mesmerize
and make him persist
So she let him in the web
she spinned

32

Of course, she gave no less than
the best
Maintain the light in this
blackness
Had him caught up in passion's flow
Even heard him screamin' *Dios Mio*
That's when she took the fatal bite
Extracted his might
So she wouldn't lose sight
And then she was done
Yup, she won
Oh, what a tangled web she's weaved
Eliminating this one before he deceived
But she possesses the power in the final hour
So she continues spinnin'
and spinnin'
and spinnin'

Watercolors and Moon Chases
(for Christine J.)

I've failed
To catch the moon
Night creatures have watched me
Paint all the stars away
It's best, I guess
Tomorrow
I'll be safe
I no longer paint flowers
For I tire of being pricked
By those scornful thorns

But colors are still around
Me
I'm glad
So I shall reach
For the lonely moon again
And I know
I will catch it

Painting is easier today
The brush is full
And with each stroke
A color gets its wings

And if vultures and wolves return
I will seduce the very part of them
That chased me away
I will be glad then

Heated!

Movin' with the stirrings of the Day Forces
I realize
The age of the Aquarian never dies
Only rise to each and every occasion
This occasion calls for an awakening
To the treachery played by those
That I chose to move with

In the calm before the storm
Thought you were a life force
Admired you in your course
Respected your choice
And as time moved on
Decided on something else

Told him the story of a love lettin' go
For me to grow
Called me Hollow
This kid named Delano
Said I wasn't shit, ain't shit, and will never be shit
Then called me a bitch
Yo, the words had me heated!

Goddamn! how time is spent
Lovin', believin', upliftin'
Things changed now that he ain't hittin' it
Truth is
It was just the union
That made him believe he was the shit
Yo, your shit made me raw
When I saw who you really are

Now that the winds have left
Peeped you in your environment
And your perceptions are made known
Expressing yourself in its negative term
Conditioned by your ignorance
Fixed with your stubbornness
Living vicariously through an old belief
The reality had me heated

But everyone's a friend, Captain
Your wicked deceit may be subtle and clever
Now I laugh at your cover
It's sad now that it's over
You can't see the truth of the matter
I'm the engaging force
The fixed metal
With a heart that lives forever
And ever
I give the love that heals shit
I'm like the Gaza strip
Adjoining the promise with the everlasting
Connecting the could be with reality
Linking heaven and earth
Creating the essence of love's birth
And relating all this with my being
This is how I weather the storm

I ain't mad atcha though
Just confirmin' what I know
That I'm the strong essence
That confuses the restless
And gives breathe to the lifeless

Supplyin' water in the desert
To the awe of the unbelieving
Give faith to the striving
Make the conniving
Forsake their treacherous ways
Just by transforming my energy
Which is connected to the God source
That you seek in your disbelief
Yo, my shit is strong
And will forever live on

Yo, you had me heated!
This is true
But peace be the words that I leave you
While I do me
And you do you
Only the best is what I bid
Hope your life is splendid

Oh yeah
Watch for me in the Sun, kid

Punk Bitch!!!

Chapter 4
Gracias Hombres, Gracias!

But Wes, I Will Remember

In the beginning was the Word.
And the Word was melodic
Reaching the Arch of Titus
Which held the beat
That was released
In the gods.
What remained of the old covenant were
People of the rhyme,
Matristic drips of air, breathing for Babylon—
Then gasping in joyance.
The Elohim of rhythms gave voice to
The repression and rebellion and
Yearnings for messianic redemption,
Remonstrating specifics of injustice.
Yes! The functions of a Jesuit.

Beat journalists and lyrical reporters
Brought to the Pharaoh
A reinterpretation of the ghetto,
Removing a people's occlusion
With the master's incredible flow.
More powerful than the second war,
Freedom of the mind became
The first line
On every itinerary that existed
In the hands of every messenger.
It was like Selassie's siege,
A promise for protensive souls that were once unheard,
And sweet was the freedom to the listener of those words!

Then came the sardonic mix,

Sporting heavy pockets but
With cotton remnants
On their fingertips.
Cold walkers who fed on the heart of Castro
And became macrocytes who
Regurgitated meaningless flows
That seeped in the marrow of the lion's shadows,
Broke the dawn in Heliopolis, city of the sun,
These lyrical pantheons
Build wayside shrines with perceived shine
Minus the gods of a conquered people.
Moral Diaspora.
Same eternal.

These were the words that gripped the neck of greatness
And caused the mango to reverse its ripeness.
The Words have become the banned book and
Threaten an ending stage of a revolution.
You see, we have a situation,
And those who think they are without obligation
Are void of methodical consecration,
And cause musical populations
To confuse the creation
With nutritional garbage,
Enforcing turbulence among the masses
And leaving minds devoid of knowledge
But full of rapid beats.
You without the beat of the verse leaves an emptiness in the
"We-ness,"
But Wes, I will remember and never forget.

Bomani Kamau
(for Rowan)

It wasn't until the Lioness looked beyond the darkness

And crossed through the thickness of their jungle

That she saw his eyes

She saw *him*—Bomani Kamau

She asked him in a very low roar,

"Bomani, what do you see?"

She looked in his eyes and saw what he saw:

He saw the tears of the sparrow

The ark of safety

And confusion of the masses.

She asked Bomani Kamau,

"What do you hear?"

She put her ear near his heart and heard what he heard:

He heard the cries of the angels

The laughter of the lilies

And the warring of the souls.

She asked Bomani Kamau,

"What do you feel?"

She touched his hand and felt his soul:

He felt the sorrow of the lost aged

The birth of victory

And the anger of the beast.

She asked Bomani Kamau,

"Reveal the source of your power."

But she found out that he kept his weapons hidden.

And you would never notice he's triumphed over the enemy every time

For he possesses a silent victory

Which even to him may not be fully understood.

After seven sunsets, the young Lioness learned from his breathing that

He overcomes the strong powers with the spirit of the most high.

His gods keep him in perfect peace,

This being an extension of his forefathers

43

And the many captains that
existed before him.

Bomani Kamau.

It was through him she won the battle of her own
loneliness.

She thinks of him and sleeps with a little more
peace

While basking in her own triumph.

I and I

(for Mr. and Mrs. Marcellus)

I was told the gods embraced your crown with glory.
I feel this when you enter my space.
And
while your arms wrap me with love,
your eyes feed me peace.

When you speak to me softly,
your voice is like sheets of song,
strong with the bass.

Strong Gods
I and I

Your angel-like frame voices your being.
It's like a buffet of power prepared by Spirit.
And
your presence whispers endurance,
loving your strength of Self.

When you pain, it's like thunderous Rain.
Emotional me, I know. But the lost tribe
is found every time you open your eyes.

Strong Gods
I and I

Lovemaking becomes a festive gathering.
I hear the beating of African drums
And
I Win with you when we
experience celebration of union.

Writing pages that complete chapters,
we become authors of an old book,
autographing each copy on the front cover.

Strong Gods
I and I

The hummingbird in my dream questions me
about this man who encourages my breathing
And
who sings the songs I give him
while clothing me with respect.

Dying ferns continue to grow
in the new planting pot on the table,
making us laugh and causing our hands to wrinkle.

Strong Gods
I and I

When I'm alone, I'm on one.
One and no one.
And
I hear sun rays as they creep
Into the cracks of my eyes.

The nourishment you give our love
ferments in my being until
I'm with you again.

Strong Gods
I and I

Thank You, Boys!

to father boy
who wasn't there when I was young
who I ran to when I got older
but ran from when he wasn't my father
I learned to forgive

and to daddy boy
who helped mommy raise me
who worked so hard outside and inside the house
I learned responsibility
(I miss you, boy)

and to ghetto boy
the first to steal my heart
who ran the streets day and night
and today has nothing to show for it
I learned that there are no shortcuts in life

and to that mean-tempered boy
who stole baby girl from me
through lies and deceit
and who beat me and told me I'm nothing
I learned that I am strong and beautiful

and to corporate boy
stiff and plain and boring
but who was nice and sorta cute
I learned to create balance

and to that older boy

who is always there when I need him
reliable, dependable just like daddy boy
I learned self-reliance
(and I love what you do with your tongue, boy)

and to wise boy
(old, wise dragon, I call him)
who keeps telling me to get myself together
and tells me I'm beautiful and smart
and tells me when I'm wrong
and admits when I'm right
and who thinks I don't have God
and who thinks I'm half crazy
and who visits me when I need *it*
I learned that—*I still like this boy!*

and to that lost boy
who refuses to find his way
and who couldn't love me 'cause he couldn't love his *Self*
I learned to love myself more

and to all the boys at the Firm
who keep me laughin'
I learned to be bullish

and to all those boys in between
who never really had a chance
I learned not to settle for just anything
and that no one can love me better than me
(but thank you for humoring me in the process!)

and to the boy who came from me
the young man

who wipes the tear from my eye
and tells me he loves me when I need to hear it most
who loves my cooking although it comes from a can
who takes care of his little sisters even when they irk his nerves
who makes me laugh with his character impersonations
who is my reason to never give up when I can take no more
who is my first seed
my first lesson
my first understanding of who I am and who I am not
I learned to raise my voice
and to keep writing 'til the hurt goes away
and I thank this boy the most
I forever love you, boy

to the sum of boys in my life
who caused me to develop who I am—
thank you

Chapter 5
Emergence
from the Ashes
*(Life: Are you ready to
die? Me: Always!)*

I *Was*—But Now I AM

I was—
But now I Am

Plastered with ugly scars—
Decorated with beauty marks

Brown garbage—
Sienna velvet

Broken, ill spirit—
A She-god *to the fullest*

Stinging from sharp glass—
Tickling from grass blades

Crawling down a dark road—
Skipping up a shade-filled path

Silent, speechless, hesitant—
Bursting with spoken word

Hopeful—
The evidence

Poor, pitiful me—
Most Amazing Self

Oh, how sweet is death!

Bloodhouse and Steel Trees

I

choking on black clouds. it
happens every day when I see
music and hear thoughts coming
from that stone gate around
ms. bessie's house. we sit on an
ivy league street amongst all the
college streets, but it's still the ghetto.

cousin trina whispers about
candy lakes and broken toys
and we laugh at black and white
holding hands in that new magazine
on mama's dresser. we peek at the
card game in the living room and smell
the fish that's frying in the kitchen

my eyelids flutter with the treble
coming from the walls I lean on
and big fat ladies scream to each
other outside stealing recipes
from the grandmothers. fireflies
suffocate in the mayonnaise jar
they're in, and we drain all the liquor
bottles when daddy joe goes to sleep.

I witness rites of passage that include
little babies creating little babies
and I hear my earth suffering the cries
from the small one sitting on the

53

cold ground.

tomorrow I'll see a man give his lady
a free trip to the concrete floor
and blue men take him away
in those shiny silver bracelets.
on Friday, I'll hear her cries for his
return amidst those beautiful brown,
black and blue eyes.

brown dots crawl around me
and trickle up my skinny legs.
big bellies keep coming out
the bloodhouse, and the music
keeps getting louder. I wonder
if I will have my turn to enter
those gates one morning.

II

Dancing with dark colors that
make up unbelief, I twist and
turn with blackness. I dip browns
and cause them to Fall. I hum
reds and admire their Glow and
change partners with blue-purples.
Then mahogany cuts in and
cuts me deep with pointed knife
in my back. I fall. And then caught
by the violets that spin me into the
bright parts of the living. The whites
take me, and I feel new and safe, and
in awe of clarity I wasn't given before.

54

I am tricked, though 'cause I never longed
to dance with the dark colors.
They were my own.

III

I am angry because my dreams take time
I am angry because no one will hear my story
I am angry because my children are rich with dreams, and mine
will hold them back—I think
I am angry because I have no money in a world where you need
money to breathe
I am angry because that nice lady can't help me because her
supervisor says she can't
I am angry because I can't help that girl realize she doesn't have to
be angry
I am angry because I don't know enough words to describe the
world around me
I am angry because I want to be honest but must lie to keep afloat

I am angry 'cause my kids may be hungry tomorrow
I am angry because I can't be happy
I am angry because I still choke on black clouds
I am angry because my destiny keeps changing without my
permission
I am angry because I keep choosing the wrong man
I am angry because the wrong man always comes with a big dick,
and that's hard to let go
I am angry cause there's not enough colors in my wardrobe
I am angry because I am angry

I am happy because I do have a dream
I am happy because the longer I live my story unfolds

I am happy because my kids' dreams are theirs and not mine
I am happy because my riches exist
I am happy because I know the gods will show the way
I am happy because the sound of music helps me comprehend
this world
I am happy because with each change, I learn more about myself
and life and the realm I live in
I am happy because I can go to any adult store and buy a dick
without a man attached to it
I am happy because the colors I have form a magnificent rainbow
I am happy because that nice lady is above the supervisor
I am happy because that other girl found her happiness
I am happy because I am happy

Open Hydrants
(for Ras)

Fighting against strong currents
Not of the sea
But under the sky
Between the wind
I become struggle

Cries from the cactus bring me
Further from the dream
Closer to the present
But deeper in the wind
I become fear

Letting go of the above
Lost in nothingness
Triumphant over reality
One with this wind
I become the waters

What seemed like an everlasting struggle
Was really a turbulent and wonderful ride with my Self

The Hand That Delivers
(for Tahjma)

I hear many voices
Some push me to good
While others lead me to bad
But they all educate my tongue
Which is why I cannot be defeated
And why I'm destroyed on the regular
It's a touchy subject for me

I have many opinions
And even more actions
But it doesn't cause even one grain of sand to move
So confusion and anger color my words
And they become my armor
Thus I became the first to test God here
But the last one to reap the repercussions
It's a touchy subject for me

I just don't care
About social contracts
And I know I should
But this grind is so damn messy
And I'm not dumb enough
To appreciate the garbage
Debated by the experts
So I become the last cell multiplying
While my sex becomes an anomaly
It's a touchy subject for me

She has more melanin than me
And I know bronze is not an element
But I refuse to be a puppet of the presstitutes

"Do xyz," they say
"Step into the light, Caroline," they say
And it's all kind of a big deal
Cuz they kill in large silent numbers
It's a touchy subject for me

Everything I do is beautiful
And everything I do is hurting
Sometimes I am painfully human
But at all times, I am dying
And when I find myself gasping for air
I notice my hands constantly working the bellows
Because lamentations cease in the breathing room
It's a touchy subject for me

Teach Me How to Cry
(for Channy)

Teach me to outcry the journey master when he lets me off at empty lots where beyond them exist oceans of internal conflict that seek to drown me

Teach me to shout when I discover the difference between the enthralling breeze from hybrid spirits and the mockingbird's faint song trying to woo me back into its nest

Teach me to yell when I forsake images of bravery for type II trauma, and the aesthetic touch from guilty hands allow my thoughts to accede earth-mother's foresight

Teach me to wail when denial in fantasy becomes ritualized through fragmented moments of intellectualization with heaven's angels

Teach me to roar when transfer points become limited boundaries made without return, and admission to life's exuberant platform is closed for the season

Teach me to hail Glory! When rigor mortis sets in my mind like a wooden log in a silk spun web, and I discover that surmounting pain only exists with the ancestral dread

Teach me how to cry completely when I encounter Self in abundance over and over and over again

Margo's Morning

My time has come
I must now regain myself
Alone
No one can hear me
Or comfort me
I feel nothing
The quietness of this place
Is unreal
I want to flee
Or have change quickly
My patience is being tried
Now
I know that for sure
I can only wait with dying fire
For things to be better
I wish I knew what lies ahead
I know if I did, I could cope
More
I don't want to cry
But I feel it coming on
I need to be held, but there is
No one to hold
Me
It is dark
I am not there but here
I wish I had traveling eyes
I would see everything
And not be afraid

Chapter 6
Awakening to New Dimensions

*(Where you call it a name,
but in reality, it has none.
Blessed be the teaching plants.)*

Check Me
(for Naomi)

Light it with blue fire
Pass it to the right
Puff and puff
Exhale
But don't inhale
Ya check?

Close your lids
Go inside the mind
Let passion flow
Take it there
Exhale
Exhale again
Ya check?

Catch the vision
Mr. Paul, do ya feel me?
See me in rhythms
Touch my hands as they glide over the keys
Listen to the fight they create
Ya check?

Come back to this place
Tell what you saw
Use adjectives, not just nouns
Laugh when it hurts to tell it
Cry if you can't feel it as you tell it
Ya check?

Light it with blue fire
Now pass it to the left
Puff and puff
Inhale
But don't exhale
Ya check?

Word Search

A search for words and
finding them not can leave one mindless
and some filled with incestuous anger.
All I find are actions playing on emotions.
La da da da

Words are not enough, and metaphors don't even come close in
the scriptures
to describe the cry of a newborn in the jaws of a pit bull,
or the laughter from evil witches and simulated gods,
or the feeling a little girl lost in rough dimensions,
or the jealous liar with power who dismisses his victim with
disregard.
Words are null in all my books. I find them not.
  Hint: Try backward in the first line

What word do we use when we are
determined but powerless in this secular world,
penniless and hungry for waters,
love-filled and then rejected by gods,
more than a woman but treated like an invisible broken doll?
  Hint: Try down (vertical) in the upper right column

What word do we use
for vibrations of pain,
and kaleidoscopes of joy,
and bountiful doses of hate,
and the repetition of this vicious cycle played on us?
  Hint: Try diagonally (east to west) in the middle section

Words are not enough, and metaphors don't even come close in
the scriptures
to describe landfills abundant with the blind and weeping,
or watching with bound hands while Grandpa is decapitated
with sharp blades,
or being overwhelmed with poisonous smoke from regal
buildings and shiny trucks,
or fist on frail bodies that break and bleed with the first blow.
Words are null in all my books. I find them not.
  Hint: Try across in the center, 3rd line from the bottom

A search for words and
finding them not can leave one mindless
and some filled with incestuous anger.
All I find are actions playing on emotions.
La da da da

That Sweet One, the Devil

Sweet Lucifer sung me a lullaby
And danced a dance of many tales.
Told me of his beginnings
And his births.
Told me of his many creations
Through the lives of those that created him.
"I live only thru those who
create me
oh! What a horrible creature some
made me
but I live, and that's what tickles me."
Sweet devil—the one that lived
In the imagination of his slaves.

Rations
(for Shawan)

Left out of many lines
Stuck with my own epidemic of self-consciousness
Full of ocean's mystery
And ready to mount St. Helen

I'm full of rhythms and melodies and tainted
With bass and decorated with the one treble
That begins this music of mine

Ready to enter other dimensions
Specific combinations come by way of wind
Narratives speak decades of the soil I tread and plow
Blocking voices of inhibitions and strange alternatives
Strange to my being

Dicing words that have false meaning
I feed them to the dogs
Why am I warring over souls?
It's rhetorical, I know
Mine belongs to me
Sometimes the most confusing Haiku

Questioning most quiet moments—
Is this the whole story?
It's rhetorical, I know
I search the portfolio of my thoughts
Having answers but doubting the reality

Breathing now
I'm reborn and feel the rations that I've been given
Are sufficient to do the job I came here to do

Wicked Joys

Six left feet struggling up steep stairs

and

white concussions make me believe it's ridiculous

and

absurd that the boy with black rubber bands in his hair gets knocked out in round three

and

again it's senseless to think that my residuals remain unclaimed after my shopping spree

and

it's silly to wish, but I do

and

my arms are not willing to share, so render me heartless

and

I know the world of chaos has run low on melanoma

and

immediately seeking wishes are the weed whackers with blunt instruments

and

now everyone is ready to rumble

and

it may sound poignant coming from a li'l imperfect girl

and

it's tempting to think of it all from a historical point of view, but it's silly to do so

and

when I tell it like this, people say it ain't my theme

and

when I turn the corner, I witness two silhouettes fighting

and

"I see," said the blind man to the deaf-mute, both of whom were politicians running for a second term

and

I don't rally for the champion because love has many faces but one eye

and

hate has many eyes but no ears

and

the death mattress is filled with mildew, but I am the spider with ten legs that can weave a magnificent web

and

this grace is bullshit

71

and

you know it's true, but it looks good when read

and

pretty when heard

and

safe to believe it is so

and

when you go through those doors, leave it unlocked 'cause I'm sure
plenty will follow

and

want to come back

and

I gotta laugh out loud when I'm in the fiction section 'cause I know
where I am

and

I don't pretend I don't

and

I love words that come to play with me

and

play with me

and

play with me, but still there isn't enough color in my wardrobe

and

now I feel romanticism is condescending because I am experiencing equal separations in unequal degrees

and

dragon, thank you for not taunting me with immeasurable doses of love.

Chapter 7
Message to the Daughters
(Sent to you from the Midheaven via fire and brimstone.)

WARRIOR!
(for Doris)

Laced with the insight of the Most High
This WARRIOR finds constant battle
Because the imposters know she is Superior
They aim to keep her in the struggle

Spirit is with this WARRIOR

Jaguar's claw endures every fight
And maintains her reign
Weakness made of bricks, resistant to kryptonite
There's no straw man in this queen

Spirit is with this WARRIOR

With the vigilant strength of Black Coffee
She awakens the dormant areas of this jungle
And with the release of her locs (the ropes of vigor)
Her might appears to double

Spirit is with this WARRIOR

Awaiting her in the land of the Canaanites, Hittites, and
Jebusites
Is a land of wine and honey
The City of David is promised to this WARRIOR
And she knows rewards are plenty

Spirit is with this WARRIOR

Although under continuous siege
She speaks victory in this wilderness
Waiting for sunlight to complete the journey
She never ceases to re-write her Script

Spirit is this WARRIOR

Meet My Daughter Purpose
(for Nia)

fair-skinned beauty
glowing in my dreams
her name means purpose

deep eyes that read volumes
into my old life
her name means purpose

hands full of Chantilly lace
placed in the sky
her name means purpose

a voice from the nebula
mixed with the cherubim's chorus
her name means purpose

a smile that dances with
colors not allowed in the rainbow
her name means purpose

smells of calla lilies
draped in new-spun silk
her name means purpose

gift-wrapped talent in trembling silver
and placed under a tree for years
her name means purpose

farewell kisses force out hidden tears

from missed moments
her name means purpose

I can't get out of bed
and always dreamin' because
her name means purpose

Lite Angel
(for Aneesah)

Smiling girl
Resilient woman
Sexy lady
Tough mother
Lite Angel

Smiling girl
Lost her job
This her sixth in two months
Cried last night
Held her child

Smiling girl
They stole her wallet
No money to pay her rent
Punched her boyfriend in the eye
Called me and told me she loved me

Smiling girl
Crashed her car
Made a new friend
Baked a casserole for her kids
Sung a song in the shower

Smiling girl
Going to the club tonight
Broke her shoe strap
Took off the other one
Danced 'til she got blisters on her feet

Smiling girl
Resilient woman
Sexy lady
Tough mother
Lite Angel

Naimah's Rock
(For Mommy. You did good, lady!)

For you, sister, I rock for your peace of mind
And for you, sister, I rock for your endurance in motherhood
And for you, brother, I rock for your struggles in happiness
And for you, brother, I rock for your quest for knowledge
And for you, sister, I rock for your pursuit to overcome
And for you, sister, I rock for your endless search for love
And for you, brother, I rock for the fulfillment of your journey
And for you, brother, I rock for your guidance and
understanding
And for you, sister, I rock for your conquering spirit
And for you, brother, I rock for the healing of your heart
And for you sister-niece, I rock for your gentle spirit
And for you, sister of my sister, I rock for your acceptance
And for you, sister of my sister, I rock for all your hopes and
dreams
And for you, Mama, my pillar of strength, I rock for your
patience with me
And your never wavering faith
Always know that I rock for you

About You

Spirit's fiesta and the soul's incense.
Original haiku in the body politic.
Breath that guides hail to the soil.
Nature's rise before the fall.
Sexual flame that decalcifies the stone.
Sweat in their brow and the yearning for home.
Treble, bass, melody, rhythm, and everlasting beat.
And you are.
Yes, yes—you are.

Made in the USA
Middletown, DE
13 February 2023

24561942R00054